W9-BNA-030

ALICE WALKER

AUTHOR AND SOCIAL ACTIVIST

SPECIAL LIVES IN HISTORY THAT BECOME

Signature LIVES

ALICE WALKER

AUTHOR AND SOCIAL ACTIVIST

by Stephanie Fitzgerald

Content Adviser: Carolyn Medine, Ph.D.,
Associate Professor,
Institute for African American Studies and
Institute for Women's Studies,
University of Georgia

Reading Adviser: Alexa L. Sandmann, Ph.D.,
Professor of Literacy,
Kent State University

Compass Point Books • Minneapolis, Minnesota

Compass Point Books
3109 West 50th Street, #115
Minneapolis, MN 55410

Printed in the United States of America.

This book was manufactured with paper containing at least 10 percent post-consumer waste.

Editor: Jennifer VanVoorst
Page Production: Ashlee Schultz
Photo Researcher: Svetlana Zhurkin
Cartographer: XNR Productions, Inc.
Library Consultant: Kathleen Baxter

Creative Director: Keith Griffin
Editorial Director: Nick Healy
Managing Editor: Catherine Neitge

Library of Congress Cataloging-in-Publication Data
Fitzgerald, Stephanie.
Alice Walker: author and social activist / by Stephanie Fitzgerald.
p. cm. — (Signature lives)
Includes bibliographical references and index.
ISBN 978-0-7565-3474-5 (library binding)
1. Walker, Alice, 1944– 2. Authors, American—20th century—Biography. 3. African American authors—Biography. 4. Social reformers—United States—Biography. I. Title. II. Series.
PS3573.A425F58 2008
813'.54—dc22
[B] 2007035560

Visit Compass Point Books on the Internet at *www.compasspointbooks.com*
or e-mail your request to *custserv@compasspointbooks.com*

Signature Lives

MODERN AMERICA

Life in the United States since the late 19th century has undergone incredible changes. Advancements in technology and in society itself have transformed the lives of Americans. As they adjusted to this modern era, people cast aside old ways and embraced new ideas. The once silenced members of society—women, minorities, and young people—made their voices heard. Modern Americans survived wars, economic depression, protests, and scandals to emerge strong and ready to face whatever the future holds.

Table of Contents

Chapter 1 Opening Night in Eatonton

On the evening of January 18, 1986, Alice Walker's hometown of Eatonton, Georgia, was awash in purple. Crepe paper decorated the store windows and a huge banner proclaimed "Welcome Home, Alice Walker."

The Pex Theater was filled with people who had each paid $10 for a ticket to the Georgia premiere of *The Color Purple*, the Steven Spielberg movie that was based on Walker's novel of the same name.

The Color Purple was Alice Walker's third novel. By the time the book was published in 1982, the outspoken, often controversial author was already well established in the publishing world. However, none of her works had attained the same level of popular and critical success as *The Color Purple*.

When the movie version of The Color Purple *was released in 1986, Walker was at work on a follow-up novel to the book.*

The Pulitzer Prize was named for 19th-century American journalist Joseph Pulitzer, who left a provision for the prize in his will. Intended to inspire excellence in the arts, Pulitzer Prizes are awarded for journalism, letters and drama, education, poetry, music, and photography.

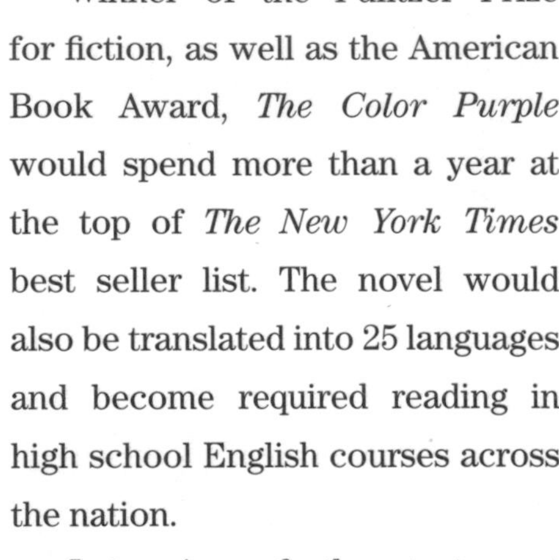

Winner of the Pulitzer Prize for fiction, as well as the American Book Award, *The Color Purple* would spend more than a year at the top of *The New York Times* best seller list. The novel would also be translated into 25 languages and become required reading in high school English courses across the nation.

Later, in a further testament to the book's popular appeal, one of America's most accomplished directors turned *The Color Purple* into a movie. Actors and nonactors alike vied for a role in the film. Comedian Whoopi Goldberg was so moved by the book that she sent a letter to Walker requesting that if the book were ever made into a film, she be considered for a part. Media personality Oprah Winfrey recalled, "I have never wanted anything in my life before or since as much as I wanted to be in *The Color Purple*."

The film had opened first in New York City on December 16, 1985, a little over a month before the Eatonton premiere. That evening, celebrities such as Quincy Jones, Bill Cosby, Arthur Ashe, Gloria Steinem, and Toni Morrison watched the movie alongside Walker and her family. In fact, it was at the

The part of Celie in The Color Purple *was only Whoopi Goldberg's second movie role.*

New York premiere that Walker's sister, Annie Ruth Walker Hood, became inspired to organize a similar event in the family's hometown. "I wanted to honor her now," Hood told reporters, "not wait until she was dead and they named some street after her."

Movie suppliers, however, did not want to release the film to a tiny theater located in a town of only 5,000 people. They insisted that the Pex Theater would receive a print of the film only after it had run in the major cities. But Walker's sister Ruth was not willing to wait. Their mother, Minnie, who had suffered a stroke a few years earlier, would only get to see the film if it came to her.

Ruth decided to go straight to the heads of Warner Brothers, the company that produced the film, and ask them to hold its Georgia premiere in Eatonton. They agreed as long as the proceeds from the evening were given to charity. Rather than turn to an existing charity, Ruth decided to create a legacy for Alice. She established The Color Purple Scholarship Fund, which provides scholarships for Georgia high school students of the arts.

Once the date for the premiere was set, Ruth went into action making sure everything was just right for her sister's big night. She could not have planned it better. That evening, as Alice Walker entered the movie theater, the crowd greeted her with a standing ovation. Minnie arrived at the theater in a special ambulance. For her comfort, a plush chair was brought from her home and placed in a prime viewing spot. Everything was arranged to let Walker and her family know how proud the town was of her accomplishment.

This special treatment was quite different from Alice's childhood experiences at that very same theater. In those days, the theater was segregated—as was every other business in Eatonton. African-Americans had to watch movies from the broken-down seats of the balcony, while white audience members could sit wherever they liked. That was part of the reason Ruth had been so eager to have the premiere at the Pex. She loved watching the theater manager bend over backward to please the very same people who had been forced to enter his theater through a door marked "colored" 20 years earlier.

Segregation might not have been on Alice Walker's mind that evening, but the recent controversy surrounding *The Color Purple* certainly was. Picketers had lined up outside during the film's Los Angeles premiere, and magazine articles had criti-

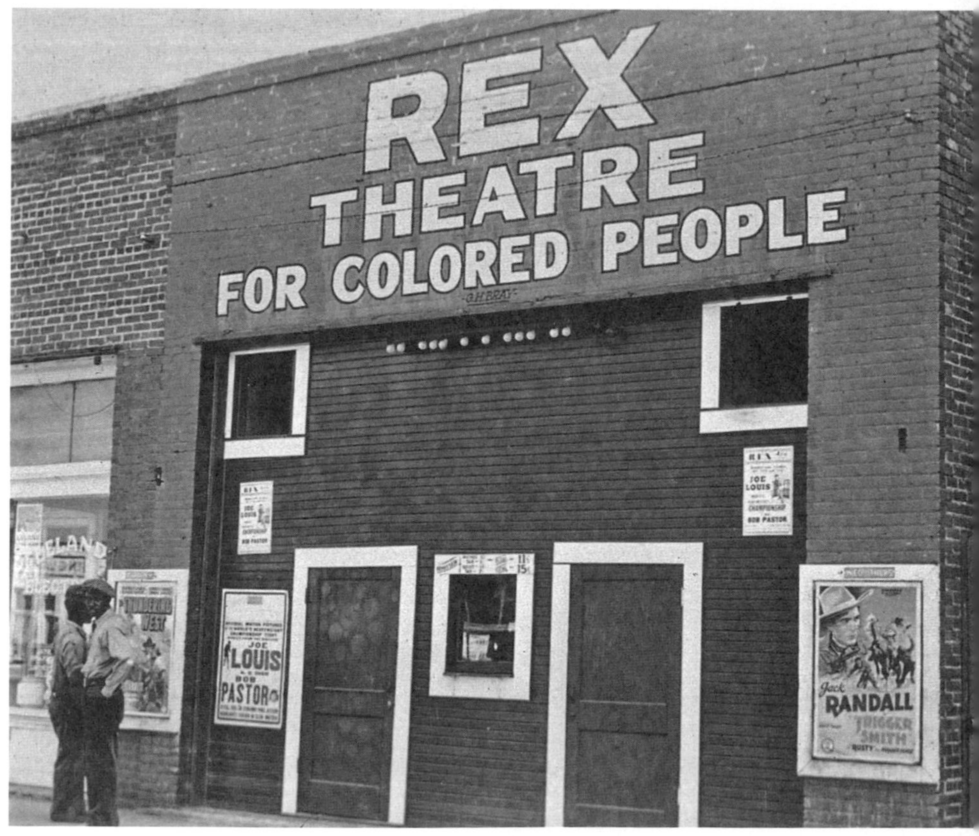

Some movie theaters, such as the Rex Theatre in Leland, Mississippi, once were specifically for African-Americans.

cized the film and the book. These people objected to the way that Walker's story portrayed African-American men—particularly the character of Mister, played by actor Danny Glover in the film. Critics argued that with so few positive African-American male role models in movies, it was irresponsible for Walker to create such an abusive, violent character.

Segregation is the practice of keeping black and white people apart. In the 19th and early 20th centuries, this separation of the races was enforced by law. During the 1950s and beyond, thanks to the efforts of groups such as the National Association for the Advancement of Colored People (NAACP), the U.S. Supreme Court struck down segregation laws one at a time. In many areas of the Deep South, though, the practice was continued whether it was within the limits of the law or not. Putting an end to this racist practice was a central focus of the civil rights movement.

Any controversy, however, was overshadowed on that evening by Walker's greatest concern: whether her mother would like the film. Minnie had suffered a series of strokes, making it impossible for her to read her daughter's award-winning book. This was one of the main reasons Walker wanted to make the film: It was the only way her mother could see her work. She need not have worried. Her mother enjoyed every minute of the film.

The author of several novels and children's books, as well as countless essays and poems, Walker had not only survived the indignities of growing up in the segregated South—she had tri-

Danny Glover played the role of Mister in the film version of The Color Purple.

umphed over them. On that special night, Alice Walker came home and was greeted as a hero, Eatonton's favorite daughter.

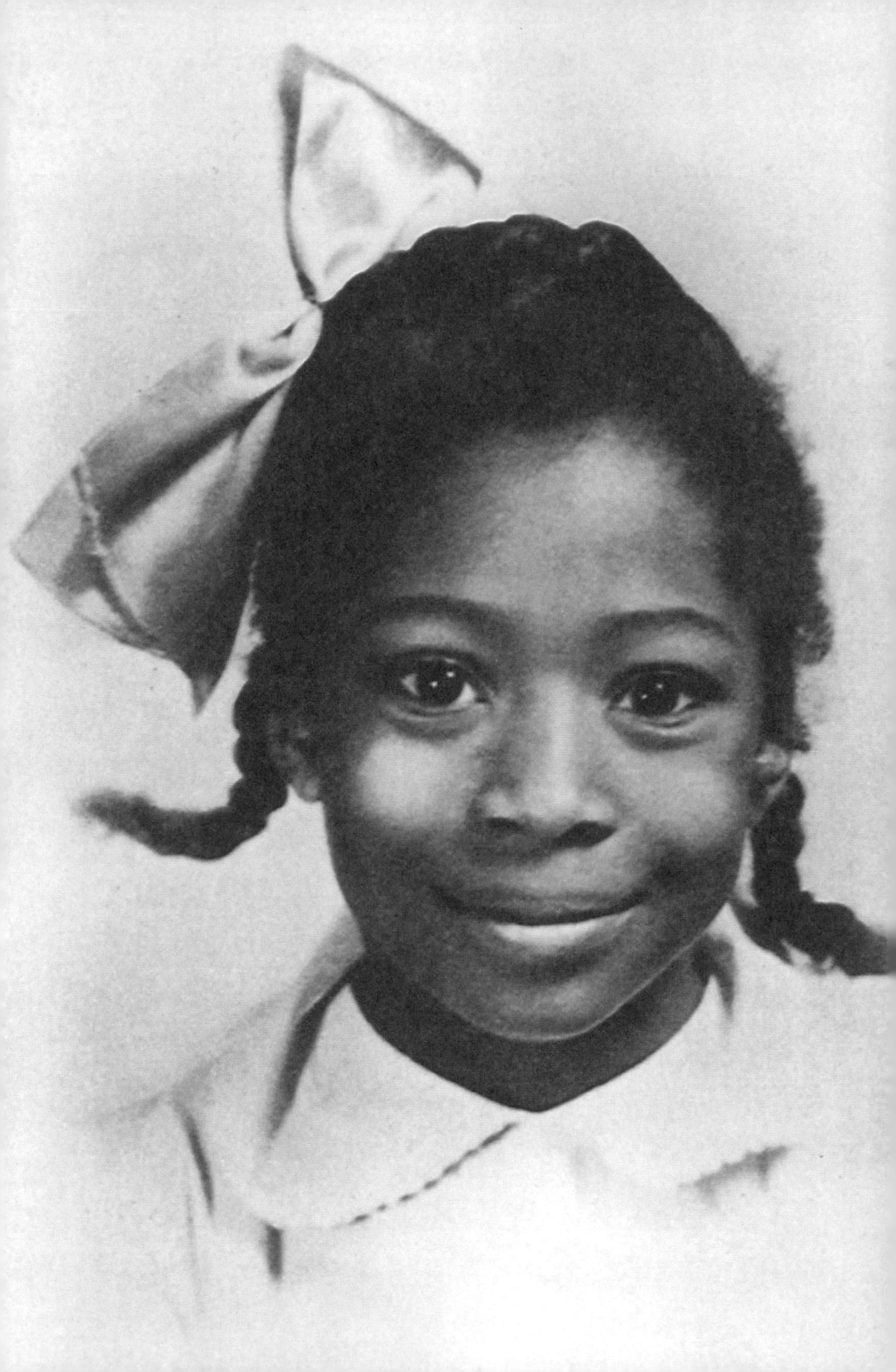

Chapter 2 It Was Great Fun Being Cute

Alice Malsenior Walker was born in Eatonton, Georgia, on February 9, 1944, the youngest of eight children. From her earliest years, Alice knew she was special. She was beautiful and bright, adored by her elder siblings and admired by the people in her community.

As a toddler, Alice would pretend to read the Sears Roebuck catalog. She would even take a twig and pretend to write notes in the margins. By the time she was 4 years old, Alice was ready to start first grade. She was certainly bright enough, according to her teacher Mrs. Reynolds, who later said that Alice was one of the smartest children she'd ever taught. But Alice's mother had another motive for starting her child in school early.

Alice Walker keeps a photo of herself at age 6 on her desk to remind her to keep faith with the child she once was.

Alice's parents were sharecroppers—they worked on plantations owned by white people. Many landlords felt that little children should join their parents in the fields as soon as they could carry a cotton sack. Minnie refused that life for her children. She believed that placing Alice in school would take her away from the influence of the landowner.

As a child, Alice was full of confidence and sass, what she calls "womanishness." Many years later, she wrote about an Easter speech she made at her church when she was 6 years old:

Sharecroppers in the early 1940s chopped cotton on rented land in Georgia.

When I rise to give my speech I do so on a great wave of love and pride and expectation. ... Naturally I say my speech without stammer or pause, unlike those who stutter, stammer, or, worst of all, forget. This is before the word "beautiful" exists in people's vocabulary, but "Oh, isn't she the cutest thing!" frequently floats my way. ... It was great fun being cute. But then, one day, it ended.

After slavery ended, many African-Americans remained on plantations where they worked the land as sharecroppers. In return for working the fields, a sharecropper would be paid a portion of the crops that he or she tended. Today many people view this practice as an extension of slavery, because the share of crops paid to the worker was usually barely enough to live on. When landowners refused to pay them their share (which was often the case), the sharecroppers had no choice but to move their families to other plantations.

The event that "ended" Alice's cuteness and shattered her sense of self was an accident that occurred when she was 8 years old. Alice was playing cowboys and Indians with two of her older brothers, Curtis and Bobby. The boys had BB guns, which they had gotten for Christmas. Alice, who had no gun and was therefore an Indian, was perched on the top of the family's garage when she felt a searing pain in her right eye. Curtis, shooting up from the ground, had accidentally shot his little sister.

Alice's brother Bill had taken the family car to work that morning, so her father and her brother

Jimmy carried the little girl up to the road. They were hoping to hitch a ride to the hospital. Mr. Walker flagged down a white driver, telling him that Alice was hurt. Jimmy later recalled that the driver did not even ask what was wrong. He just gave the trio a dirty look and continued on his way.

Back at the house, Alice's parents examined her eye. Alice later wrote:

> *I close my left eye while they examine the right. There is a tree growing from underneath the porch that climbs past the railing to the roof. It is the last thing my right eye sees. I watch as its trunk, its branches, and then its leaves are blotted out by the rising blood.*

For one week, the family treated Alice's injury with home remedies. Alice lay in bed, crushed with pain, as a thick white scar formed over her eye. Finally, the Walkers found a doctor in Macon who agreed to treat Alice's eye. He wanted $250 up front—almost as much money as Alice's parents made in a year.

Bill was able to borrow the money from his boss, but it quickly became clear that he had wasted his time. The Macon doctor barely looked at Alice after pocketing the money. Then he made a statement that would haunt the young girl for most of her life.

He claimed that eyes were "sympathetic," and since Alice's right eye was blind, she would soon lose her sight in the left eye, too. For many years, Alice was terrified by the prospect of going completely blind.

After the accident, Alice became withdrawn and solitary. She spent hours walking through the fields and the woods where she lived. At home, she spent much of her time in her room reading and filling notebooks with her writings. The accident that had left Alice blind in one eye had an unexpected benefit: It set her on the path to becoming a writer.

As a child, Alice lived in Putnam County, Georgia.

It would be many years before Alice would recognize another positive side effect of her injury. She said:

> *It really made me understand how blind most people are because they have their two eyes, they don't have any fear of blindness, and they often just don't see anything, it seems to me. They take everything for granted. They never seem to realize the wonders that are all around them at every possible moment. They don't see trees, they don't see the sky, they don't take a minute to really be appreciative of all that seeing is. Seeing takes us into life in the most amazing way.*

Bill always believed that the Macon doctor took so little interest in Alice's case because she was a poor, black sharecropper's daughter. It was a belief that had its basis in the harsh realities of life for black people living in the segregated South.

From the time she was young, Alice knew that the world was a different place for a black child in the South than it was for a white child anywhere. All she had to do was look around her: White people lived in the nicest houses. Black people lived in shacks, and they did not even own those. She realized that people like her parents worked all year for the white people, and the white people did not work at all, or

A woman stood outside a shack, which she shared with a number of other black sharecroppers and their families.

so it seemed. "Even if nobody laid it out verbally," she said, "it was just a … knowing that this could not possibly be right."

Though the family was poor, Alice's mother brought beauty to their life in many ways. After a long day spent working in the fields or in someone else's home, Minnie would cook for the family using the fruits and vegetables that she raised in her own garden. In the evenings, she would sew clothing and quilts that would keep her children warm in winter.

Walker wrote about her youth in the country: "Perhaps my Northern brothers will not believe me when I say there is a great deal of positive material I can draw from my 'underprivileged' background. But they have never lived, as I have, at the end of a long road in a house that was faced by the edge of the world on one side and nobody for miles on the other. ... In the cities it cannot be so clear to one that he is a creature of the earth, feeling the soil between the toes, smelling the dust thrown up by the rain, loving the earth so much that one longs to taste it and sometimes does."

Somehow, every day Minnie even found time to tend her garden, which was home to more than 50 varieties of flowers.

Alice later recalled:

> *My mother was my salvation. She was extremely tired, having had eight children and working from sunup to sundown in the fields and in other people's kitchens. So when she would come home and work in her garden, which was her special thing, I would go out to be with her and we would just walk among her flowers and hold hands and hug. That little time together made all the difference in my growing up.*

No matter how many times the Walker family moved, or where they lived, there were always flowers. Minnie was famous for her gardens, and they had a healing effect on Alice. She told a reporter from *U.S. News & World Report:*

> *I couldn't move anywhere without my eye hitting flowers. So, on the one hand, there*

was this awful system of exploitation ... and broken spirits and, on the other, this incredibly sustaining natural beauty. I was shortchanged by society, but abundantly fed by nature.

Still, Alice always knew that, like her siblings, someday she would have to leave the South to escape the oppression that had been so much a part of her life. She would later write:

I was an exile in my own town, and grew to despise its white citizens almost as much as I loved the Georgia countryside. But I would have to leave all this. Take my memories and run north. For I would not be a maid, and could not be a "girl," or a frightened half-citizen, or any of the things my brothers and sisters had already refused to be.

Chapter

3 The Gifts of Family

One by one, Alice's siblings had moved north. Her eldest sister, Mamie, had left Eatonton when she was 13 years old because there was no high school for black students in their town. When Mamie came back to visit, she gave Alice a glimpse of a better life—one that was not constrained by "whites only" restaurants and theaters, or by schools that used cast-off equipment and old textbooks from white schools.

Alice's beloved brother Bill had also moved north. Just as soon as he was able to repay his boss' $250 loan, Bill moved to Boston in search of a better life. In the summer of 1958, when Alice was 14, Bill was once again looking for a way to ease his baby sister's pain.

Alice wrote to Bill often, telling him of her

During Walker's childhood, African-American children in the South attended segregated schools.

When she was young, Alice considered becoming a scientist. She liked the idea of being able to help people. The only microscope available to black students, though, was a broken cast-off from the white school. "So that meant that when I got to thinking about being a scientist, there was no way I could do that in a school that had one broken microscope," Alice later explained.

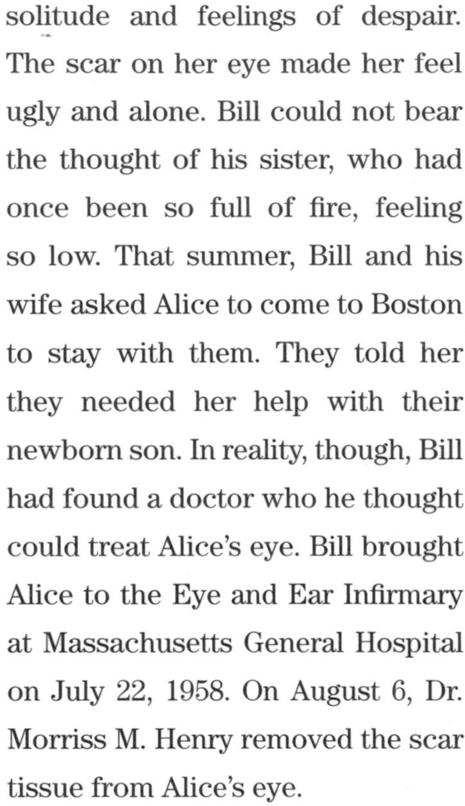

solitude and feelings of despair. The scar on her eye made her feel ugly and alone. Bill could not bear the thought of his sister, who had once been so full of fire, feeling so low. That summer, Bill and his wife asked Alice to come to Boston to stay with them. They told her they needed her help with their newborn son. In reality, though, Bill had found a doctor who he thought could treat Alice's eye. Bill brought Alice to the Eye and Ear Infirmary at Massachusetts General Hospital on July 22, 1958. On August 6, Dr. Morriss M. Henry removed the scar tissue from Alice's eye.

After the operation, Alice felt like a different person. Though she remained permanently blind in her right eye, the removal of the scar tissue transformed her personality. She went on to be voted most popular in her high school, and she was also crowned senior prom queen and named valedictorian of her class.

During this time, Alice also started to resist the limitations of segregation and discrimination. According to classmate Bobby Baines, "Alice never accepted the lowly station of blacks in the South. She

The Massachusetts Eye and Ear Infirmary is associated with Harvard University.

was conscious of the injustices long before the rest of us recognized them and started to fight."

By the mid-1950s, the civil rights movement was gathering steam. In 1955, Rosa Parks' refusal to give up her seat on an Alabama bus sparked the Montgomery Bus Boycott and gave African-Americans a leader to rally behind: Dr. Martin Luther King Jr.

The modern civil rights movement began in the 1950s, as African-Americans worked together to gain equality with whites. Various groups emerged to fight the battle on several fronts. The NAACP used the court system to challenge unjust laws. Groups such as the Southern Christian Leadership Conference and the Student Nonviolent Coordinating Committee staged protests and marches to call attention to unfair practices.

Martin Luther King Jr. was a Baptist minister who was quickly recognized as one of the most important leaders of the civil rights movement. An advocate of nonviolent resistance, King dedicated his life to the cause, braving racist attacks, police brutality, and time in jail in his fight for equal rights for African-Americans.

One afternoon in October 1960, Alice was sitting in front of the family's first television set with her mother when she saw Dr. King for the first time. In fact, it was the first time she had ever seen a black person on TV.

Alice watched as King was placed in a police car. He was being arrested for leading a protest against the segregated lunch counters in an Atlanta department store. Alice later recalled:

> *Seeing the footage of Dr. King getting arrested was definitely a turning point. He showed me that black people were no longer going to be passive and just accept the inhumanity of segregation. He gave me hope.*

After his arrest, Dr. Martin Luther King Jr. (center) passed through a lunch counter picket line on his way to the courthouse. He was escorted by Atlanta Police Captain R.E. Little (left rear).

King also helped Alice understand how important it was for black people to stay in the South and fight for change rather than running north. When she graduated from Butler-Baker High School, Alice chose to stay in Georgia and attend Spelman College in Atlanta.

Once again, Alice's eye injury provided an unexpected gift. She received a scholarship from the Georgia Department of Rehabilitation, which was available to students with disabilities. The scholarship provided free textbooks and half of her college tuition. Because of her excellent grades in high school, Alice received a second scholarship, this one from Spelman College, which covered the other half of her tuition.

Rosa Parks' refusal to give up her seat on a Montgomery, Alabama, bus on December 1, 1955, led to the first big protest of the civil rights movement. After Parks was arrested, civil rights leaders formed the Montgomery Improvement Association to organize a boycott of the city's bus system. The boycott lasted one year, during which more than 40,000 African-Americans stayed off the buses. On November 13, 1956, the U.S. Supreme Court declared segregation on buses illegal, and on December 21, African-Americans started riding the buses once more.

People in the community raised an additional $75 to help Alice with her college expenses. Alice's mother, however, provided the most meaningful gifts once again. Minnie gave her daughter three things she herself had never owned: a suitcase, a typewriter, and a sewing machine. These gifts, Alice believed, were her mother's way of giving her child permission to travel.

As she boarded the bus that would take her to Atlanta, Alice was reminded of what her choice to stay in the South would mean. Inspired by Rosa Parks, Alice chose to sit in the front section of the bus. After a white woman complained, the bus driver told Alice to move. Alice's father had come to the bus station to see her off. Only the

Rosa Parks took her first ride on a desegregated Montgomery public bus in December 1956—more than a year after she refused to give up her seat to a white man.

knowledge that he might be harmed if she objected kept Alice from speaking out. But as she later wrote, "In those seconds of moving, everything changed. I was eager to bring an end to the South that permitted my humiliation."

Chapter

4 A Change Is Going to Come

Alice Walker's political activism began in earnest when she reached Spelman College. She joined the Student Nonviolent Coordinating Committee and took part in demonstrations in downtown Atlanta every Saturday morning.

The summer after her freshman year of college, Walker was invited to the World Youth Peace Festival in Helsinki, Finland. It was the first time she had ever left the United States. Women from Atlanta's African-American churches raised the money for Walker and another student to travel to Finland. Before they left, they got the chance to meet with Martin Luther King Jr.'s wife, Coretta Scott King.

In 1963, the summer after her sophomore year, Walker was again staying with Bill in Boston, working

Dr. Martin Luther King Jr. gave his famous "I Have a Dream" speech at the 1963 March on Washington for Jobs and Freedom.

The proposed Civil Rights Act of 1963 was not signed into law until 1964. The law made racial discrimination illegal in public places, such as theaters and restaurants, and required employers to offer equal job opportunities to African-Americans. It also stated that projects involving federal funds would lose their funding if there was evidence of discrimination on the job.

to save money for school. In August, she took a bus to Washington, D.C., to take part in the March on Washington for Jobs and Freedom. The event had been planned to call attention to the high unemployment rate among black people and to bring attention to a civil rights bill that was awaiting President John F. Kennedy's signature.

More than 200,000 people—black and white—participated in the March on Washington on Thursday, August 28. Because of the crowd, Walker was unable to get close to the speakers standing at the foot of the Lincoln Memorial. From her perch on a tree branch, though, she could hear every word. For Walker, as for everyone gathered there, the highlight of the day came when King delivered his "I Have a Dream" speech.

The young woman was particularly struck by one part of King's speech, which would stay with her forever. He said:

> *I am not unmindful that some of you have come here out of great trials. … You*

> *have been the veterans of creative suffering. Continue to work with the faith that unearned suffering is redemptive. Go back to Mississippi, go back to Alabama, go back to South Carolina, go back to Georgia, go back to Louisiana, go back to the slums and ghettos of our northern cities, knowing that somehow this situation can and will be changed.*

Walker had never heard anyone encourage black people to "go back to Mississippi." In her experience, the only path to change was on the road heading north. As she later wrote, "I knew if this challenge

Marchers carried signs demanding social and economic justice for African-Americans.

were taken up by the millions of blacks who normally left the South for better fortunes in the North, a change couldn't help but come."

Nevertheless, after the first semester of her junior year, Walker found herself heading north. It was time to leave Spelman. She felt the school was too "opposed to change, to freedom, and to understanding that by the time most girls enter college they are already women and should be treated as women."

Staughton Lynd, a former Spelman professor, agreed with Walker's impressions of the school. He later explained:

Alice Walker spent time with her parents on their front porch during a visit home from college.

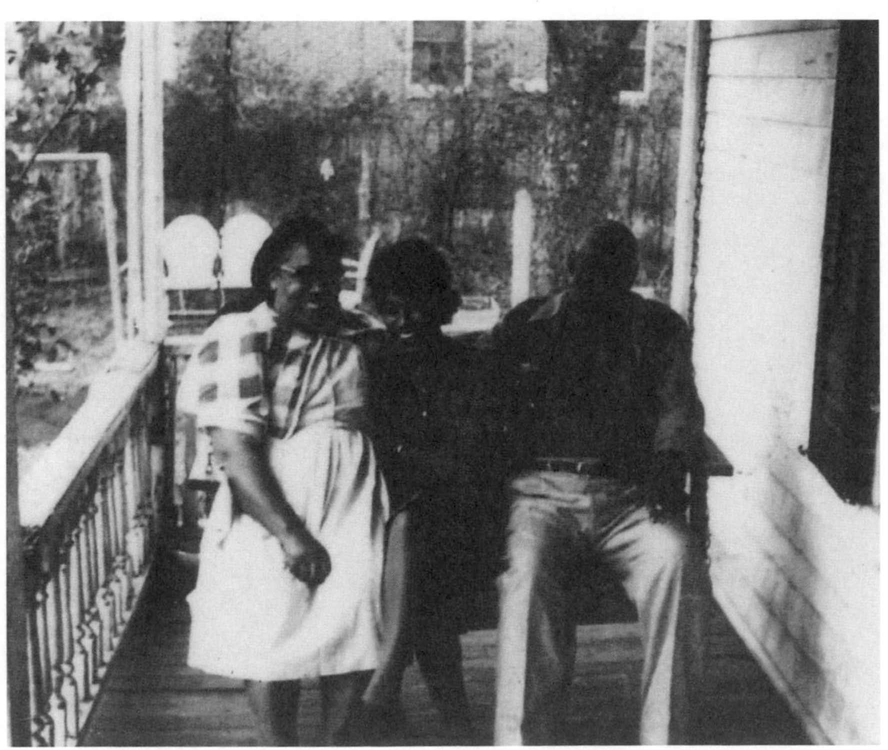

The students would go downtown and picket segregation and then come back to this walled-off campus with ... rules put in by a generation of black administrators who were basically helping to keep Jim Crow [segregation] alive.

After receiving a scholarship to Sarah Lawrence College in Bronxville, New York, Walker left Georgia. Suddenly she found herself in an almost completely white environment. She had gone from an all-black school to one where she was one of only six people of color.

Being a minority on campus did not hinder Walker, who really began to find her voice as a writer at Sarah Lawrence. She later said:

I had written at Spelman, but very few people seemed to care. For the most part, writing was considered decorative. At Sarah Lawrence everybody understood that writing was about your heart and your soul and you did it because you had to. ... I was consumed by my work. It was wonderful.

She also found an important mentor and advocate in Muriel Rukeyser, a poet and faculty member at the school. With every piece that Walker wrote, it became clearer that she would one day be an important literary talent.

But a trip to Africa in 1965 almost derailed Walker's ambitions. She had gone to Kenya that summer as part of a foreign study group called the Experiment in International Living. While there, she worked on a pineapple plantation and helped build a schoolhouse. She also had a relationship with a man there and became pregnant.

When she returned to Sarah Lawrence in the fall, Walker was in despair. She believed that motherhood was not right for her at the time. She felt she could not have the baby, but abortion was illegal, and she did not believe she had other options. With no money and no connections to a doctor who could perform the procedure, Walker fell into a depression. She considered suicide and slept for three nights with a razor under her pillow. Just when Walker had made peace with her decision to commit suicide, a classmate found a doctor who would perform an abortion.

Following her procedure, Walker's emotions came out in a rush of poetry. She wrote for a full week, stopping only to eat, sleep, and go to the bathroom. Walker has said that during this period and for years after, her poetry was fueled by depression. Though that has since changed, this process taught her about the value of sadness. She reflected:

> *There's no point in wanting life or anything to be all cheery and bright all*

Walker drew on her sadness to create her poetry.

the time, because in that cheeriness and brightness we don't learn all that much. We're too busy having a great time and enjoying it, which is wonderful too. But when we have to go very deep into pain and suffering, sadness, it's very possible that our own feelings are trying to inform our intelligence—sending a message from the emotions to the brain. And poetry is riding on that.

Every morning, Walker would slide a new batch of poems under Muriel Rukeyser's door. Walker later said that she did not care what Rukeyser did with her poems. She just wanted someone to read them. As it turns out, Rukeyser sent the poems to her agent, who in turn sent them on to an editor at a publishing house. The collection of poems, about Africa, suicide, and life in the South, was accepted immediately. The poems were published in a collection titled *Once* three years later, in 1968.

Muriel Rukeyser (1913–1980)

At the time that she was working on her poems, Walker also wrote a short story called "To Hell with Dying." The story is about an old man named Mr. Sweet. Broken down by life and heartache, Mr. Sweet is about to die. But each time he lies on his deathbed, a neighbor brings his children to see Mr. Sweet and says, "To hell with dying, man, these children want Mr. Sweet!" The children then tickle and kiss Mr. Sweet back to life.

Like many characters and situations in Walker's

writings, Mr. Sweet was a man whom she had really known as a child. Walker had heard about the real Mr. Sweet's death while she was in college. She could not afford to go home for his funeral, so she remembered him in her own way—with a story.

Alice shared the short story with Rukeyser, who passed it on to the author Langston Hughes. Two years later, Hughes published "To Hell with Dying" in a book titled *Best Short Stories by Negro Writers.* The story was also published as a children's book in 1988.

Langston Hughes was a great American writer whose work celebrated African-American culture and racial pride, promoted equality, and condemned racism. He was one of the most influential artists of the Harlem Renaissance, an African-American artistic movement in the 1920s that celebrated black culture. Hughes' huge body of work includes poetry, novels, plays, essays, and children's books.

Chapter 5 Into the Fire

When Alice Walker graduated from Sarah Lawrence in January 1966, no one in her family was at the ceremony. But she was not discouraged. She was 21 years old and ready to start her writing career in earnest. She moved to New York City and took a job as a caseworker with the welfare department. For a writer just starting out, the job was a good way to pay the bills. Walker also appreciated the chance to help people.

But Walker's job took an enormous toll on her writing. The strain of her job made it almost impossible for her to be creative. After six months, Walker quit. In a lucky twist of fate, soon after leaving the welfare department, Walker received a writing grant of $2,000. Her original plan had been to go to Senegal,

An African-American man registers to vote for the first time in Marion, Alabama, after the Voting Rights Act of 1965 was passed.

West Africa, to write. But recalling Martin Luther King Jr.'s encouragement to go back to Mississippi, Walker decided she was most needed at home in the United States. She joined the National Association for the Advancement of Colored People (NAACP) Legal Defense and Educational Fund (LDF) in Jackson, Mississippi.

At that time, Mississippi was a dangerous place for African-Americans. In a region where oppression and violent racism were the norm, Mississippi stood out as the worst offender. It was just this bloody and brutal reputation that made Walker want to go there.

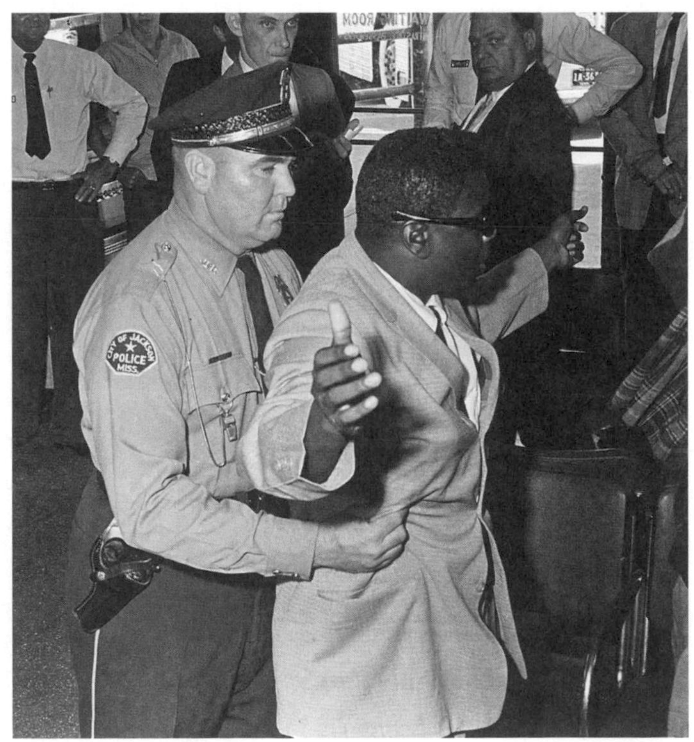

On May 29, 1961, more than a dozen African-American activists were arrested in Jackson, Mississippi, after attempting to integrate the local bus station.

She later explained:

> *All my life Mississippi had been the epitome [greatest example] of evil for black people. I knew that if I was to be able to live at all in America, I needed to be able to live unafraid, anywhere. I had to face up to the system that had almost done me in and so many of my people. Mississippi was the test.*

When Walker arrived in Jackson, she was introduced to Mel Leventhal, a law student from New York who was also working with the NAACP LDF. Leventhal, who was white, had no idea what he would be up against when he decided to go to Mississippi. He later explained:

> *If I had ever studied up on exactly how dangerous it was to try to end segregation in Mississippi, I might not have had the courage to go. I could not have imagined the level of racism down there. My ignorance is what saved me.*

Some of the most brutal crimes against black people were committed in Mississippi. From 1882 to 1962, 538 African-Americans were lynched in Mississippi—more than any other state in the country. It was also the place where 14-year-old Emmett Till was taken from his uncle's home and killed by a group of white men who did not like the fact that Till had spoken to a white woman. Medgar Evers, an NAACP field officer in Mississippi, was gunned down in the driveway of his home. Civil rights workers Andrew Goodman, Michael Schwerner, and James Earl Chaney, who came to Mississippi to register voters, were killed by a group of white supremacists that included the county sheriff.

It was decided that Walker and Leventhal would work together taking depositions from black people in Greenwood, Mississippi, who had been evicted from their homes when they tried to vote. Even though the 15th Amendment guaranteed African-Americans the right to vote, many states used tricks to keep them from the voting booths. Some black people were forced to take literacy tests or pay a poll tax when they tried to register to vote.

On August 6, 1965, President Lyndon Johnson had signed the Voting Rights Act into law. The Voting Rights Act made poll tax and literacy tests illegal, but

Surrounded by members of Congress, President Lyndon Johnson signed the Voting Rights Act of 1965 into law in a ceremony in Washington, D.C.

some states found other ways to keep black people from the polls. People in Mississippi and other states used intimidation and the threat of violence to keep black people from voting. The stories Walker and Leventhal gathered would be used in a lawsuit against the state of Mississippi.

As they worked together over the summer, the mutual respect that Walker and Leventhal had for one another turned to love. Not only were interracial relationships dangerous in Mississippi, they were also against the law. However, this couple, who had endured harassment from Mississippi police and been chased through darkened back roads by white supremacists, would not be discouraged. At the end of the summer, Walker brought Leventhal home to Eatonton to meet her parents. Mr. and Mrs. Walker were impressed with Leventhal and liked him very much—though they did not realize at the time that the two were romantically involved.

White supremacists believe that white people are superior to all other races. In fact, these racists look at black people as if they were less than human—and treat them that way. The Ku Klux Klan is an infamous group of white supremacists that made it a practice to harass, abuse, and even kill black people. It also set its sights on white people who supported African-Americans, such as civil rights workers.

After their summer in the South, Walker and Leventhal moved to an apartment in New York City. During their time in Mississippi, Walker had allowed Leventhal to read some of the poems from *Once*. He was extremely moved by her writing and did everything to encourage it. Knowing how important it was for Alice to be surrounded by nature as she worked, Leventhal set up a writing table for her in front of a window that overlooked Washington Square Park. They covered the table with a colorful bedspread, which they topped with an earthenware jug that was always kept full of flowers. It was at this table, pounding away on the keys of the type-

Washington Square Park is an oasis of green in New York City.

writer her mother had given her, that Walker began work on her first novel. This novel, titled *The Third Life of Grange Copeland*, was about a poor sharecropper's family from the South.

Walker has a unique way of writing. She never sits down and tries to think of a story idea. She explains:

> *Patience is fundamental in creation. And so I'm very patient and I will wait years for something to be fully formed. Because to me sitting down and thinking that I want to do something that's not really present in my emotions is almost unthinkable. My feeling is that that would be like chasing it. Running after it with a net to capture it when it's not really ready to be with me.*

When Walker has an idea for a story, she waits for the characters to "visit" her. As the characters develop in Walker's mind, they tell her about themselves. Then she lets their stories unfold as quickly or as slowly as they need to. She usually sets aside a year or two to focus on the project at hand. She does not necessarily need to write for a year straight, but as she explains:

> *I need to hold a place for it [the story] to come. It's like cleaning out a house so*

that if I am to have guests, when they do arrive, everything is perfectly placed and situated for their comfort and for their long stay if they wish to stay long.

As winter descended on New York City, the characters in Walker's novel grew silent. She felt that they did not like the cold. Walker took a break from the novel to write an essay on the civil rights movement for a national writing contest. The essay, titled "The Civil Rights Movement: What Good Was It?" won first prize. The piece, which was Walker's first published essay, ran in the autumn 1967 issue of the magazine *American Scholar*.

"The Civil Rights Movement: What Good Was It?" was an answer of sorts to people who questioned how much had been accomplished by the movement. In the essay, Walker admits, "Materially, it [the movement] provided them with precious little that they wanted." But she goes on to list the immaterial gains that African-Americans got from the movement:

If knowledge of my condition is all the freedom I get from a "freedom movement," it is better than unawareness, forgottenness, and hopelessness, the existence that is like the existence of a beast.

Leventhal later recalled that Walker wrote the entire essay in one sitting. He said:

> *The essay had come to her in full form, and it was magnificent. She may have tinkered with it a little, but what you see on the printed page is pretty much what she handed to me straight out of the typewriter.*

African-Americans gathered to demand their civil rights in 1966's March Against Fear.

Walker confirms that she's not the type of writer who wastes a lot of paper. She says:

> *I've never been a writer who did a lot of editing and correcting on the paper, but I do an awful lot of that in my mind. I think that goes back to having been in a*

large family and needing to protect my space and my thoughts and whatever I was creating.

Walker was finished with her essay, but the characters from her novel did not return. It seemed to Walker as if they did not like the city—they were country people. Luckily Walker had been accepted for a writing residency at the MacDowell Colony in Peterborough, New Hampshire. For six weeks, Walker stayed secluded in her cabin, finishing several chapters of her book.

Leventhal came to visit every weekend. He was going to graduate from law school in the spring, and then he would return to Mississippi. Walker left her writing residency to join him. Although she never really believed in marriage as an institution, she proposed to him before they left. Walker and Leventhal were very much in love, but Walker had political as well as romantic motives.

For years a law had existed in Mississippi that made it illegal for black and white people to intermarry. Just three months before Walker and Leventhal moved to Mississippi, the U.S. Supreme Court had declared the law unconstitutional. Changing a law does not automatically change people's attitudes, though. By going to Mississippi as a married couple, Walker and Leventhal would be making a statement about equality. "We intended to stand our ground," Walker later remarked. "We came to Mississippi to kill the fear it engendered [caused] as a place where black life was terrifyingly hard, pitifully cheap."

The couple married on March 17, 1967. They bought a home in Jackson, Mississippi, and settled down to their work—Mel as a civil rights attorney, Alice as a writer, crafting more poems, stories, and her novel. Always aware of the danger that surrounded them, they bought a large dog for protection and kept a loaded gun by their door.

Walker has lived in many locations in the United States.

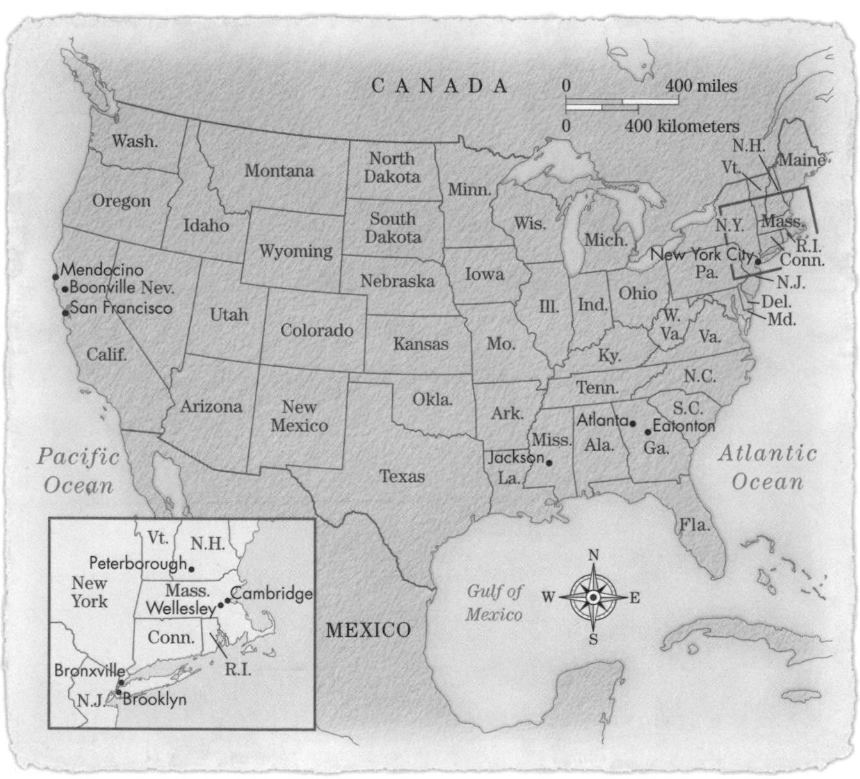

Alice Walker during her time in Jackson, Mississippi

Despite the constant threat of violence, Walker thrived as a writer. She was eager to tell the stories of the African-American women whom she met in Mississippi. Through her work as a consultant in black history for the Friends of the Children of Mississippi (FCM), Walker got that opportunity.

Walker's job at FCM was to develop a history curriculum for teachers in the Head Start program. She later wrote:

I came to my job filled with enthusiasm. These were women I identified with, women who'd do anything for the good of black children. ... I felt, on my first day before my class, as if the room were full of my mothers.

Walker decided that the best way to teach these women black history was to have them examine their own personal histories. She asked them to write their own autobiographies. The funding for Walker's position was withdrawn before long, but Walker had gained from the shared experience. What she learned from the women in her class would help shape much of her writings in the coming years.

Chapter 6

Joy and Pain

In the fall of 1968, Walker's first book of poetry, *Once*, was published. This significant achievement came on the heels of an emotionally trying time for Walker and Leventhal.

Earlier in the year, the couple had learned that Walker was pregnant. Although initially concerned about how a baby would affect her writing, Walker soon took joy in the idea of starting a family. In mid-April, however, she suffered a miscarriage—the result, she believes, of the terrible sadness she felt over the assassination of Martin Luther King Jr. on April 4.

Walker and Leventhal made the trip from Jackson to Atlanta to take part in King's funeral. Together with 200,000 other mourners, the couple walked for

On November 17, 1969, Alice Walker and Mel Leventhal welcomed their daughter, Rebecca, into their family.

In April 1968, Martin Luther King Jr. was in Memphis, Tennessee, to campaign for better wages and living conditions for sanitation workers. The day before he was assassinated outside his motel room, he gave a speech that seemed to foreshadow his death: "Like anybody, I would like to live a long life. Longevity has its place. But I'm not concerned about that now. ... I may not get there with you. But I want you to know tonight, that we, as a people, will get to the promised land! So I'm happy, tonight. I'm not worried about anything. I'm not fearing any man."

four miles (6.4 kilometers) behind King's casket, which was carried on a mule-drawn wagon. One week later, Walker had her miscarriage. She later wrote, "I did not even care. It seemed to me, at the time, that if 'he' (it was weeks before my tongue could form his name) must die no one deserved to live, not even my own child." It was King's widow who would eventually give Walker the strength to carry on.

At the end of April, Walker saw Coretta Scott King on television. Mrs. King was in New York to deliver a speech. It had only been three weeks since her husband's death, but she was up and working. During her speech, King said that she thought her husband would have wanted her to speak in New York despite her grief. She spoke about how important it was for her to continue his work.

Watching King on television gave Walker strength. She started to think that her own grief was just self-pity. It was time to get back to work. As often happened in her life, Walker used her craft to

Two hundred thousand mourners followed King's casket along the funeral procession route in Atlanta, Georgia.

pull herself out of depression.

Soon Walker was writing again and teaching classes at Jackson State University. In 1969, she found out she was pregnant again. On November 17, her daughter, Rebecca, was born—three days after Walker finished writing *The Third Life of Grange Copeland.*

Published in 1970, the book tells the story of a poor black sharecropper. The title refers to the three stages of Copeland's life that are shown in the book. In the beginning of the story, Copeland's desperate life of poverty has caused him to become a bitter, abusive man. He drinks and fights with his wife and eventually leaves his family. When his wife kills herself, the couple's son, Brownfield, is left alone.

The second stage of Copeland's story takes place in the North. There he spends his time beating up as many white men as he can. Over time, though, Copeland begins to see that he cannot blame white people for all his problems. He begins to develop a sense of self-worth.

When Copeland returns to the South to be with his son, he discovers that the young man is repeating his pattern of abuse. Brownfield brutally murders his wife and is sent to prison. Copeland takes on the responsibility of raising his granddaughter Ruth. He finally has the chance to be the good father that he was not able to be to Brownfield. When Brownfield is released from prison and tries to take Ruth back, Copeland kills him.

The Third Life of Grange Copeland was greeted with mixed reviews. Critics liked the book, but many people felt that Walker was unfair in her portrayal of men. It was a criticism that Walker would hear for years to come.

Meanwhile, three years in Mississippi was taking its toll on Walker. Of course there was the hatred and racism—the bus driver who called her "girl," the day care workers who didn't want to look after any "black kids," the constant threats and slurs aimed at her and her husband. Walker also felt her creativity drained by the lack of culture in Jackson. She longed for theater and the symphony and for other artists with whom she could share her thoughts.

Finally, in September 1970, Walker applied for a writing fellowship at the Radcliffe Institute in Cambridge, Massachusetts. While she waited for a response, Walker taught classes at Tougaloo College and worked on her second novel.

Walker received the Radcliffe fellowship, and by September of the next year, she and Rebecca were living in Cambridge. Leventhal stayed in Mississippi to continue his work for the NAACP.

Radcliffe was a women's college until it became part of Harvard University.

Soon after Walker began her residency at Radcliffe, she landed a job at nearby Wellesley College, where she designed a course on black women writers. Walker, who deeply appreciated the inspiration she had gained from these artists, realized that their work was largely ignored on college campuses.

But between the demands of motherhood and her teaching position, Walker could not devote as much time as she would have liked to her own writing. Rebecca also was suffering in the cold

Rebecca with her doll in 1973

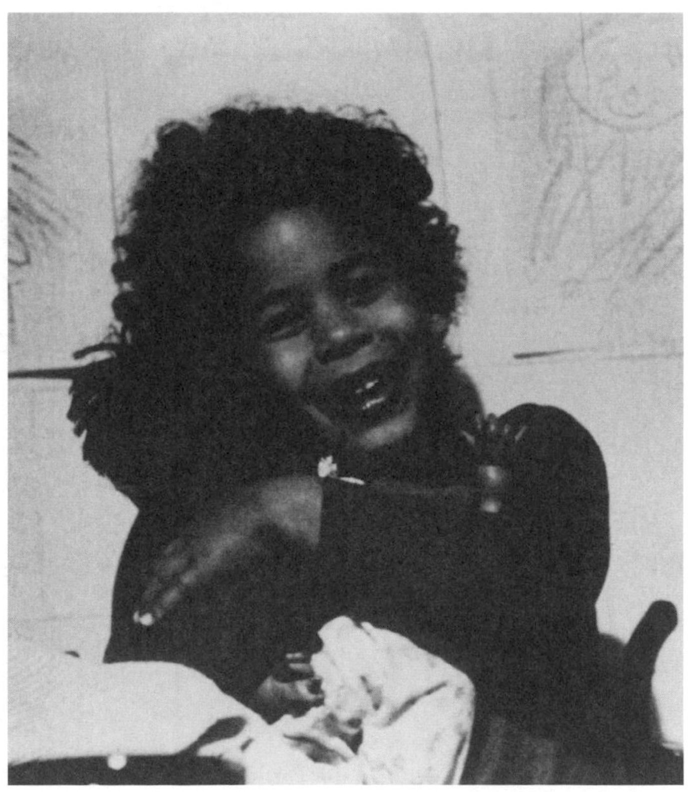

climate of New England. After a winter marked by one illness after another, Walker and Leventhal decided that their daughter would be better off with her father in the warmer climate of Mississippi.

Walker had mixed emotions about the arrangement. She was unhappy about being apart from Rebecca, but she knew that being alone would allow her to finish her new novel within a year. After all, in the time she had been in Cambridge, even with her many responsibilities, she had managed to finish a second volume of poetry. In fact, *Revolutionary Petunias & Other Poems* had already been accepted for publication.

Today Walker's daughter, Rebecca, is co-founder of the Third Wave Foundation, a national activist organization for young women ages 15–30. Named one of the 50 influential leaders under 40 in 1994 by Time *magazine, Rebecca is also a published author. In her 2002 memoir,* Black White and Jewish: Autobiography of a Shifting Self, *Rebecca shares her memories of growing up caught in the middle of two worlds—and never really feeling completely whole in either.*

All through Walker's childhood, a lavender petunia bloomed in her family's yard. No matter how many times the Walkers moved, no matter how many times Walker's mother dug up that petunia and replanted it, it always survived. Thirty-seven years after she first planted the petunia, her mother gave a piece of it to Walker.

When Walker was writing the poem "Revolutionary Petunias," she thought about that plant and how it

Her mother's lavender petunia plant became for Walker a symbol of the strength of African-American women.

seemed so much stronger than modern petunias. It reminded her of the strong black women she knew, and she wrote about them in the introduction to the collection: "These poems are about … (and for) those few embattled souls who remain painfully committed to beauty and to love even while facing the firing squad."

Another poem from *Revolutionary Petunias & Other Poems* is called "For My Sister Molly Who in the Fifties." The poem is about Walker's sister Mamie, who left home at age 13 to go to school. Although she came back to visit as often as she could, the better educated Mamie became, the more she seemed to distance herself from her family. It seemed to Alice that her sister was ashamed of her family—that she thought they did not speak or dress properly and that their house was shabby and run-down.

Walker started out writing an angry poem. However, as she wrote draft after draft—something she rarely does—Walker began to understand her sister's feelings. She understood that Mamie had begun to see the family through the eyes of her college friends.

Walker worked on "For My Sister Molly Who in the Fifties" for five years and wrote more than 50 drafts. The final version speaks only of the good things that Mamie shared with her younger sister, not the sense of abandonment that Alice could not have helped but feel.

As her fellowship drew to a close, Walker applied for, and received, an extension. She would remain at Radcliffe for the 1972–1973 school year.

In 1973, her debut collection of short stories, called *In Love & Trouble: Stories of Black Women*, was published. Although that year was a good one for Walker professionally, it started out on a sad note personally. On January 26, 1973, Walker's father, Willie Lee, died. He was only 63. At her father's funeral service, as Walker stood in front of her father's casket, she heard her mother say, "Good night, Willie Lee, I'll see you in the morning, without smiles, without tears, without regrets."

Walker's parents, Minnie and Willie Lee, in a 1930s portrait

In 1979, Walker would publish another book of poetry, which she titled *Good Night, Willie Lee, I'll See You in the Morning.*

When she finished her residency at Radcliffe, Walker returned to Mississippi, but she was not prepared to stay for long. Though Leventhal wanted to stay and continue his civil rights work, he realized that to save his marriage he would have to leave the South. In 1974, Alice, Rebecca, and Mel moved back to New York. Nevertheless, Walker and Leventhal's marriage would dissolve within two years.

With Walker's return to New York came a new job opportunity. Gloria Steinem, the founder of *Ms.* magazine, offered her a position as a contributing editor at the magazine. Not willing to let her art suffer, Walker agreed to take the job only if she could limit her time in the office to two days a week and not be required to attend any meetings. Steinem was happy to accommodate Walker, who used her time outside the office to work on her first children's book, a biography of author and poet Langston Hughes.

Walker had met Hughes for the first time in 1967, when he published her short story "To Hell with Dying." The two connected immediately, and Hughes became Walker's mentor and friend. Before meeting the writer, Walker had never read any of his work. When she admitted as much to Hughes, he responded by giving her an armful of his books. That day, Walker promised herself that one day she would write a book for children about Hughes. Seven years later, in 1974, her book *Langston Hughes: American Poet* was published.

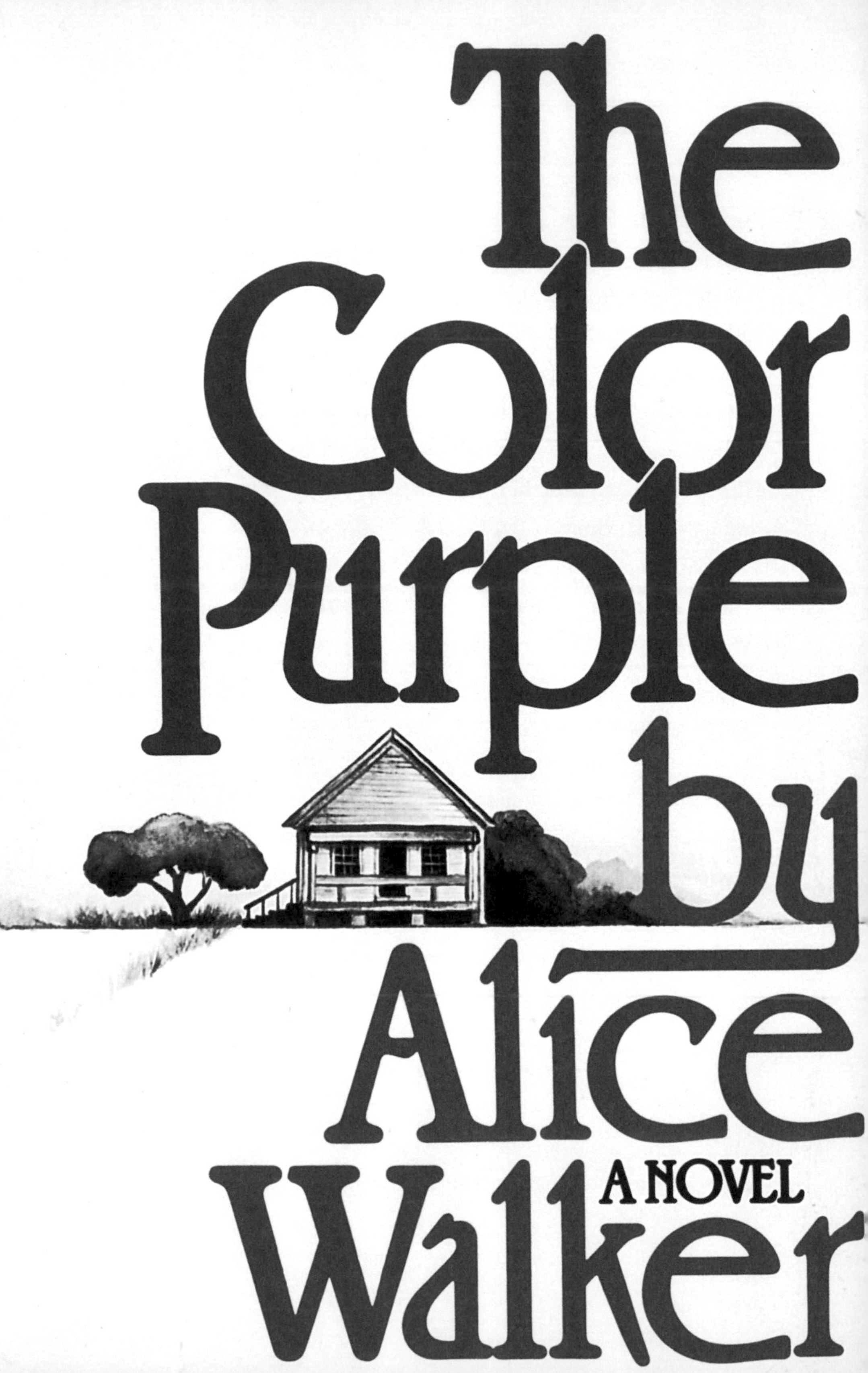
The Color Purple
by
Alice Walker
A NOVEL

Chapter 7 THE COLOR PURPLE

When Alice Walker left Mississippi in 1974, she had the draft for her second novel, *Meridian*, in hand. The novel, about the role of women in the civil rights movement, was published in 1976. Because there were many similarities between the title character of the story and Alice Walker, many people thought the book was autobiographical.

Walker explained that the book was not autobiographical, but that there was a part of her in all her characters. "I'm everywhere and I'm everybody," she once told an interviewer. "That's true in all my books."

After completing *Good Night, Willie Lee*, and sending it to her publisher, Walker edited a collection of works by Zora Neale Hurston titled *I Love Myself*

The first edition of Alice Walker's novel, The Color Purple, *was published in 1982.*

Zora Neale Hurston was a novelist, folklorist, and anthropologist who was an important figure in the Harlem Renaissance. At a time when African-Americans were being encouraged to blend into white society, Hurston stood out by embracing and celebrating her blackness. The outspoken and flamboyant writer is best known for her 1937 novel Their Eyes Were Watching God, *which was made into a television movie in 2005.*

When I Am Laughing ... And Then Again When I Am Looking Mean and Impressive. Then she started on another novel, *The Color Purple.* She had gotten the idea for the story while walking with her sister Ruth. The sisters were talking about people they knew who were involved in a love triangle. That conversation was the spark that Walker needed to get her new novel started.

During this time, Walker had moved to Park Slope, a neighborhood in Brooklyn, New York. In an effort to bring country life to Brooklyn, Walker had planted a tree in her front yard and one in the back. She was trying to create a space where the novel's characters would come to her and, more important, where they would be comfortable enough to stay.

After three months, Walker realized she could not stay in Park Slope. She believed that the characters in her new book did not seem comfortable there. Walker needed silence in order to let her characters develop fully.

In 1978, Walker sold her house in Park Slope and

Walker's home in Park Slope

moved to San Francisco. Walker quickly realized that San Francisco was still too busy for her work. Her characters, she decided, were country people. After exploring the region, Walker found a place in Boonville, a small community in northern California that felt like her own Georgia home.

Though she believed this was a place where her characters could feel comfortable, she still did not feel they were fully satisfied. *Ms.* magazine had kept Walker on staff after she moved, so she was still working for the magazine from home. In addition to her magazine duties, Walker was often crisscrossing the country to give readings and lectures. It soon became clear that Walker's characters needed her complete attention. She would have to drop everything and focus on this book.

Walker found her new home in Boonville, California, to be a better place to write.

Ms. offered to continue paying Walker even though she was taking a leave of absence. Walker had also recently sold her second collection of short stories, *You Can't Keep a Good Woman Down*. The book would not be published until 1981, but the advance payment from the publisher plus her *Ms.* salary would enable Walker to write for a year.

Ms. magazine was co-founded in 1971 by Gloria Steinem, a writer and important leader in the women's movement. For more than 30 years, the magazine has focused on women's issues, such as discrimination in the workplace, abortion rights, sexual harassment, and other feminist causes.

Walker settled into her country home, started on a quilt, and took long walks outside. As the weeks passed, her characters came to her and began telling their stories. Walker thought it would take her five years to finish the book, but she ended up finishing it within a year. *The Color Purple* was published in 1982.

As the story opens, the reader is introduced to Celie, a 14-year-old girl who is raped by her mother's husband. At the time, Celie believes this man is her father, though it is discovered later that he is not. The man warns her not to tell anyone but God what has happened. With no one else to turn to, Celie begins to write letters to God.

At first, Celie's situation seems hopeless. After giving birth to two children who are taken from her,

> *Celie writes her letters to God in what Walker calls "black folk English." Walker has a great love for this, the language of her parents and grandparents, because she feels it is direct and to the point. Walker does not like the word dialect, which she calls racist. She says that when authors write in a dialect, they use a lot of apostrophes and contractions—what she interprets as their need to show that they really know how to spell the words correctly.*

she is forced to marry a widower who is verbally and physically abusive and who treats her like a servant. It is only after Celie meets and falls in love with her husband's mistress, Shug Avery, that she begins to develop some sense of self-worth.

The novel is full of characters modeled after people Walker knew. In some ways, Mister is like her grandfather, who was hard and abusive as a young man but who mellowed later in life. Shug reminds Walker of her aunts who lived up north. When they visited the Walkers, Alice's aunts were always beautifully dressed and full of fire. The character of Sophia, who has incredible strength and forthrightness, brings to mind Walker's mother, Minnie.

The novel contains themes that many people found disturbing—including rape and violence. The strange thing is that critics did not seem to be disturbed that these things existed in the world. They were disturbed that Walker had written about them. Part of what makes Walker's writing so compelling, though, is its honesty. She writes about things she has

Walker sat with her mother, Minnie, who held a photograph of herself and her husband from the 1930s.

seen and does not hide the truth to satisfy critics.

When Walker finished writing *The Color Purple*, she wept. She had grown to love the characters so much that she knew immediately that she would miss them terribly once they were gone.

With the book behind her and Shug, Celie, and Sophia gone, Walker returned to teaching. She also resumed her travels, appearing around the country for poetry readings and lectures. But the enormous success of *The Color Purple* would soon change Walker's life dramatically.

Walker's novel was on *The New York Times* best-seller list for more than a year. It would ultimately sell more than 5 million copies and be translated into 25 languages. The novel also won the American Book Award and the Pulitzer Prize for fiction, making Alice Walker the first African-American woman to receive that honor.

Walker later compared the success of *The Color Purple* with what it felt like to be named valedictorian and crowned senior prom queen in high school. But her feelings about receiving the Pulitzer were not as clear.

She said that when an author she liked received an establishment award, one given by an organization, it made her stop reading their work. She also commented that she "would've felt happier if I'd gotten such a prize from the women in my mother's church. Because I know those women, and I know that they have high standards."

In addition to awards and praise, Walker was also receiving many more requests to give personal appearances and interviews. Her fans wanted to know more about her. All of these commitments made it difficult for Walker to pursue her craft. In an effort to answer some of her fans' questions, Walker published a collection of essays, speeches, and reviews. Called *In Search of Our Mothers' Gardens: Womanist Prose*, the book was published in 1983 and serves as Walker's autobiography.

Walker grew vegetables and flowers at her California home.

At the beginning of In Search of Our Mothers' Gardens, Walker introduces the term womanist. At that time, many black women and other women of color did not feel connected to the feminist movement, which they viewed as a middle-class white women's movement. Their experiences with oppression were very different and included racism and classism in addition to sexism. Walker created the word womanist to describe their perspectives and experiences. She wrote, "Womanist is to feminist as purple is to lavender."

At about the same time, Walker was working on her fourth book of poetry. *Horses Make a Landscape Look More Beautiful*, published in 1984, was a bit of a departure for Walker. To that point, she had been writing stories about the trials and triumphs of African-American women. The poems in *Horses Make a Landscape Look More Beautiful* focused on two main themes—the environment and Walker's non-black heritage.

Walker has Native American ancestors and white ancestors. She had no problem identifying with her Native American ancestors. In her opinion, Native Americans and African-Americans shared a lot of the same experiences at the hands of white Europeans.

Walker had a difficult time coming to grips with her white heritage, however. Walker's great-great grandfather on her father's side was a white slave owner who raped one of his slaves—Walker's great-great grandmother. Walker wrote a poem called "Family Of" about her great-great grandfather. In

"The Thing Itself," she writes about the actual rape.

As Walker grappled with these issues of identity, Hollywood came calling in the person of Steven Spielberg. The famous director wanted to make a film adaptation of *The Color Purple*.

Walker's ancestors (here, her four grandparents and their children) are a source of inspiration for much of her writing.

Chapter 8 In the Glare of Hollywood's Lights

Alice Walker did not know anything about Steven Spielberg, who had directed *Jaws*, *Raiders of the Lost Ark*, and *E.T. The Extra-Terrestrial.* When she was first approached about the idea of making her book into a film, Walker was not sure it was something she wanted to do.

Walker felt that African-Americans had not been well represented by Hollywood. However, learning that Quincy Jones would be a co-producer on *The Color Purple* eased her mind a bit. Jones had written the score for the miniseries *Roots*, which Walker loved. He was also responsible for putting together the USA for Africa benefit, which raised money for famine and disease relief. For these reasons, Walker believed that he had a good heart. She also came to

Oprah Winfrey played Sophia in the film version of The Color Purple, *a character Walker says is based on her mother, Minnie.*

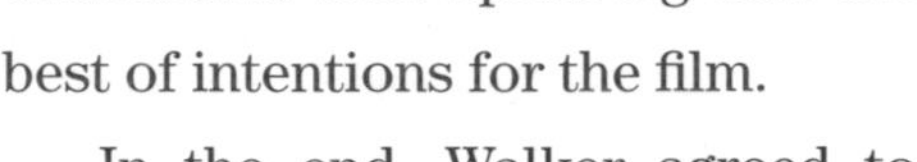

understand that Spielberg had the best of intentions for the film.

In the end, Walker agreed to make the movie mostly because she saw it as an opportunity to reach a wider audience. Her experiences during the civil rights movement had shown her that change was possible. A person's ability to change—and to triumph over hardship—was a central theme in her book. She wanted to share that message with as many people as possible.

Before agreeing, though, Walker insisted that at least half of the crew be composed of women and minorities. The producers readily agreed. As actress Whoopi Goldberg, who played the role of Celie, later proclaimed, "There had never before been that many black folks involved in every aspect of a major release."

Walker also wanted a hands-on role in the production. Usually when an author's book is adapted into a film, the writer has no say about how the movie is made. But Walker, who was unwilling to relinquish total control of her creation, even had a

Quincy Jones, called "Q" by his friends, started his musical career as a teenager, teaming up with a young singer named Ray Charles. Throughout the 1950s, Jones wrote music for and played with such legendary performers as Count Basie, Duke Ellington, and Dizzy Gillespie. Jones has written the music for more than 30 movies, as well as the theme songs for such landmark television series as The Cosby Show. *Jones has been nominated for more Grammy awards than any other artist, and he has won 26.*

Whoopi Goldberg, as Celie, took instructions from director Steven Spielberg.

say in selecting the cast.

Still, Walker chose to lend her name to the production only as a consultant. As is the case for authors in most screen adaptations of books, Walker did not have real control over the movie that Spielberg ultimately made. As she later explained:

> *No matter how good his intentions, I feared that Steven's version of* The Color Purple *might not be worthy. I wanted it to be clear to the ancestors that I'd tried to honor them as best I could. Beyond that, the movie was out of my realm.*

Walker was given an opportunity to write a script for the film adaptation, but her draft was never used. Instead, producers used a screenplay written by Dutch writer Menno Meyjes. When she was on the set, however, Walker helped Meyjes by suggesting rewrites for scenes that were not working.

The first time Walker saw the film, she watched it in a nearly empty theater, and she did not love it. She told a reporter:

> *The first time I saw it, I was in this theater with about two other people, and it looked funny. It sounded funny, and I thought everybody was a cartoon. So I went to the premier thinking, "This is a very brave thing to do since you think this is a terrible film." But you know, there in that theater, with hundreds of other people, it was a wonderful film. I really enjoyed it. It's not the book, but the fact is Quincy Jones and Steven Spielberg did their best. They loved it and they worked really hard.*

Although the movie did well at the box office and earned 11 Academy Award nominations, including one for Best Picture, it was surrounded by controversy. As in the past, Walker was criticized for her portrayal of African-American men. She was also criticized for allowing a white person to direct the film.

She later said:

Much of the criticism of The Color Purple *has to do with Walker's portrayal of African-American men, as in the character of Mister, played by Danny Glover in the film version.*

The people who have criticized me on this need to get clear on the fact that Steven is the only one who asked to make the movie. Steven was limited in what he understood about life in America for black people. But he has a good heart, and he was trying to be accountable.

The author is not much concerned with how critics view her work. She explains, "I'm doing what I'm here to do. I think critics have to criticize, and I have to write. We're even!"

Chapter

9 Doing What I'm Here to Do

Using the money she made from *The Color Purple*, Alice Walker purchased a 40-acre (16-hectare) retreat near Mendocino, California. She planted 100 trees and several gardens, creating a beautiful and peaceful retreat that perfectly suited her love of nature and need for silence. For a woman who had been raised on borrowed land and forced to move almost every year at the whim of a white landlord, owning her own property was a dream come true.

Also on the property were the offices of Wild Tree Press, a small publishing company that Walker founded with two partners. In keeping with her commitment to activism, Walker vowed only to publish books that showed political awareness. She also vowed only to publish books that she loved.

Walker compares her role as a writer to that of a tree bearing nuts or fruit.

The house at Walker's "Wild Tree" retreat

Through the years, *The Color Purple* continued to affect Walker's life and work. In 1989, she published *The Temple of My Familiar*, a book she had worked on for eight years. The book focuses on three couples and takes place in Europe, Africa, and the Americas. It also brings back characters from *The Color Purple*, including Celie and Shug.

In 1992, Walker published *Possessing the Secret of Joy*. This novel also features a character from *The Color Purple*. This time it is Tashi, an African woman who is married to Celie's son, who is the main character of the novel. Like many women from Africa, the

Middle East, and Southeast Asia, Tashi is subjected to circumcision in the book.

In female circumcision, the practitioner removes all or part of a young girl's external genitalia. The procedure is performed while the child is awake, without any pain medication, and usually using unsterilized tools. People claim that the procedure is done to make young women more "marriageable." Critics of the practice believe it is done to keep women from enjoying sex.

Walker had heard about female circumcision when she traveled to Africa in the early 1960s. It was a topic she had always wanted to write about, but it took her more than 20 years to figure out the best way to do so.

Before *Possessing the Secret of Joy* came out, not many people had spoken out against the practice of female circumcision. Now the topic was getting a lot of attention. Still, Walker felt she needed to do more. In 1993, together with British-Indian filmmaker Pratibha Parmar, she produced *Warrior Marks*, a documentary about female circumcision.

Once again, Walker's actions attracted criticism. Some people felt an American had no business telling people in other countries how to live. Although she rarely spoke publicly about criticisms she received, this time Walker could not remain silent. She said:

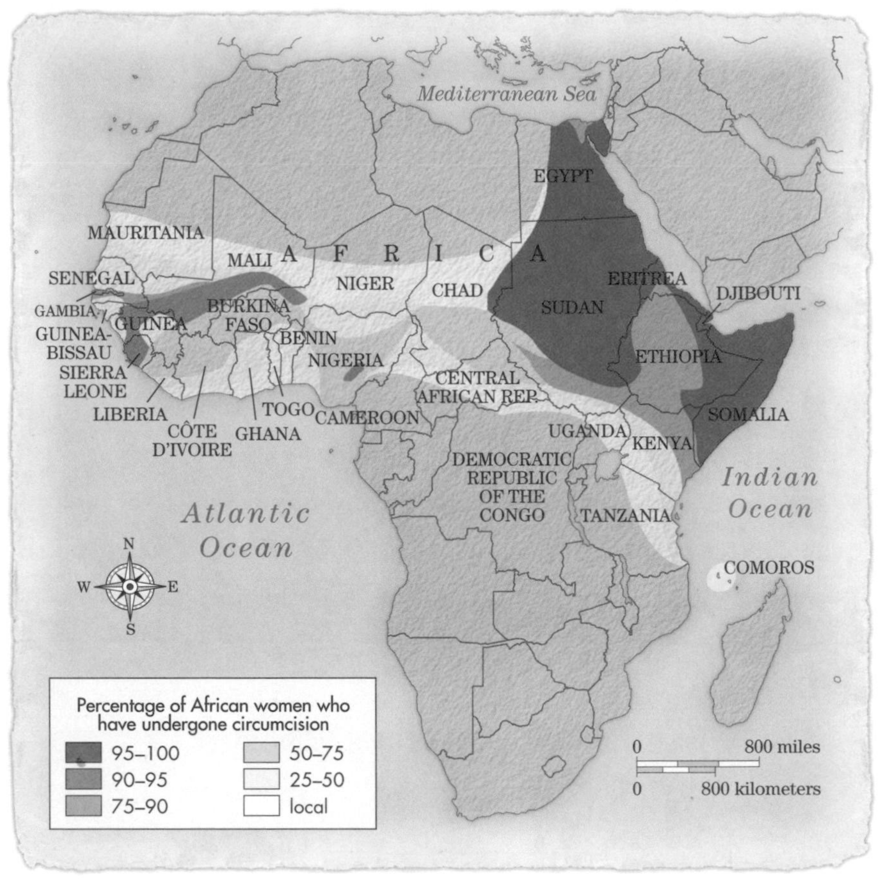

Female circumcision is a cultural practice across much of Africa.

As far as I'm concerned, I am speaking for my great-great-great-great grandmother who came here with all this pain in her body. In addition to having been captured, put in the hull of a ship, packed like sardines, put on the auction block, in addition to her children being sold, she being raped, in addition to all this, she might have been genitally mutilated. I would go nuts if this part of her story weren't factored in.

Thanks to public backlash against the ritual, in July 2001, officials from nearly 200 countries agreed to a United Nations resolution rejecting the practice.

In 1996, Walker revisited *The Color Purple* in a different way. *The Same River Twice: Honoring the Difficult* looked back on Walker's experiences with the film adaptation of her book. *The Same River Twice* includes Walker's journal entries and personal correspondence from that period, as well as the unused screenplay that Walker wrote for the film.

As these works were being published, Walker continued to create children's books and collections of her poetry and essays. As always, her writings showcased the themes and causes that were closest to her heart.

Then, in 2000, Walker published a collection of stories titled *The Way Forward Is with a Broken Heart*, which included a rare look inside the writer's private romantic life. "To My Young Husband" looks back at Walker and Leventhal's forbidden love.

After the book was published, Walker said she saw *The Way Forward* as the result of a 30-year writing cycle and that the collection might be her last original work. She said she had other things she wanted to do with her life.

Walker has definitely done other things, supporting the causes she believes in and speaking out against the things that she does not. Walker also has continued to write. In 2004, she published another novel, *Now Is the Time to Open Your Heart.* In 2006, her children's book *There Is a Flower at the Tip of My Nose Smelling Me* was published, as well as a collection of essays and speeches titled *We Are the Ones We Have Been Waiting For: Inner Light in a Time of Darkness.*

The Color Purple, however, continues to be the work for which Walker is best known. In 2005, a stage adaption of the novel opened on Broadway. When asked whether she is concerned about the success of her later works and how they will compare with *The*

Alice Walker, with Oprah Winfrey, addressed the audience on opening night of The Color Purple *on Broadway.*

Color Purple, Walker's response is exactly what one would expect:

> *What do you think? I'm doing what I'm here to do. It's like any tree out there, they're producing whatever they're doing, maple leaves and figs and pears and apples, and that's what I'm doing. And I do it at my own pace, and I do it as it comes to me to be done. And I'm happy when other people enjoy it or learn or whatever it is they do, but I've had that experience. I've had the experience and the joy of creating something. And I don't really wait around or worry about the reception particularly. I'm happy when it's well received; of course it makes me happy. It's like when you give someone a gift and they say, "Oh, this is wonderful, I could really use this," as opposed to someone who says, "Oh God, another tie, another pair of socks."*

For the millions of fans who will always say, "I could really use this," Alice Walker's writings continue to inspire.

Life and Times

Alice Walker's Life

1944
Born February 9 in Eatonton, Georgia

1952
Accidentally shot and blinded in the right eye by a BB gun pellet

1961
Graduates as valedictorian from Butler-Baker High School; wins a scholarship to Spelman College

1950

1944
Operation Overlord begins on D-Day with the landing of 155,000 Allied troops on the beaches of Normandy, France; it is the largest amphibious military operation in history

1953
Sir Edmund Hillary of New Zealand and Tenzing Norgay of Nepal are the first two men to reach the summit of Mount Everest

1961
Soviet cosmonaut Yuri Gagarin is the first human to enter space

World Events

1966

Graduates from Sarah Lawrence College; moves to New York City and works for the welfare department; moves to Mississippi to work for the NAACP LDF

1967

Marries Mel Leventhal, a civil rights attorney, on March 17; wins first prize in a national writing contest for her essay "The Civil Rights Movement: What Good Was It?"

1968

First book of poetry, *Once*, is published; becomes writer-in-residence at Jackson State College

1965

1966

The National Organization for Women (NOW) is established to work for equality between women and men

1968

Civil rights leader Martin Luther King Jr. and presidential candidate Robert F. Kennedy are assassinated two months apart

Life and Times

Alice Walker's Life

1969

Daughter Rebecca is born November 17

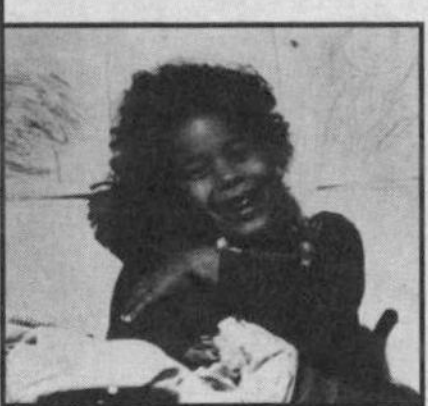

1970

First novel, *The Third Life of Grange Copeland*, is published; becomes writer-in-residence at Tougaloo College; awarded Radcliffe Institute Fellowship

1974

Moves to New York City; becomes an editor at *Ms.* magazine; first children's book, *Langston Hughes: American Poet*, is published

1970

1969

U.S. astronauts Neil Armstrong and Edwin "Buzz" Aldrin are the first people to land on the moon

1971

The first microprocessor is produced by Intel

1973

Spanish artist Pablo Picasso dies

World Events

1976

Is divorced from Mel Leventhal; novel *Meridian* is published

1979

Good Night, Willie Lee, I'll See You in the Morning, a book of poems, is published; edits a collection of works by author Zora Neale Hurston titled *I Love Myself When I Am Laughing … and Then Again When I Am Looking Mean and Impressive*

1982

Novel *The Color Purple* is published

1980

1976

U.S. military academies admit women

1978

The first test-tube baby conceived outside its mother's womb is born in Oldham, England

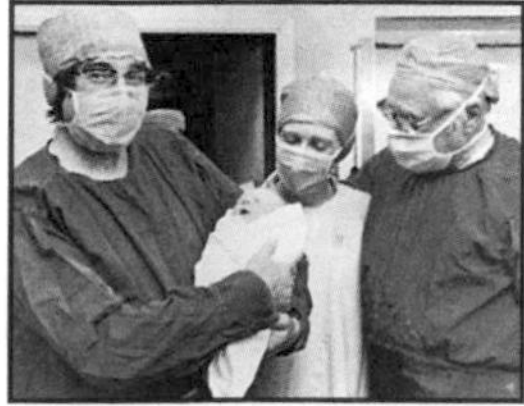

1982

Maya Lin designs the Vietnam War Memorial, commemorating Americans who died

Alice Walker's Life

1983
Awarded the Pulitzer Prize for *The Color Purple; In Search of Our Mothers' Gardens: Womanist Prose* is published

1984
Launches Wild Tree Press; fourth book of poetry, *Horses Make a Landscape Look More Beautiful*, is published

1985
Film version of *The Color Purple* premieres

1985

1983
Sally Ride becomes the first American woman to travel in space

1984
U.S. scientists isolate the virus that causes AIDS (acquired immune deficiency syndrome), which will become a world-wide epidemic

1986
The U.S. space shuttle *Challenger* explodes, killing all seven astronauts on board

World Events

1992

Novel *Possessing the Secret of Joy* is published

2000

The Way Forward Is with a Broken Heart, a collection of stories, is published

2006

There Is a Flower at the Tip of My Nose Smelling Me, a children's book, and *We Are the Ones We Have Been Waiting For: Inner Light in a Time of Darkness*, a collection of essays and speeches, are published

2000

1991

The Soviet Union collapses and is replaced by the Commonwealth of Independent States

2001

September 11 terrorist attacks on the two World Trade Center Towers in New York City and on the Pentagon in Washington, D.C., leave thousands dead

2007

Former Vice President Al Gore and a United Nations panel on climate change win the Nobel Peace Prize for their efforts to spread awareness of global warming

Life at a Glance

Date of Birth:	February 9, 1944
Birthplace:	Eatonton, Georgia
Father:	Willie Lee Walker (1909–1973)
Mother:	Minnie Tallulah Grant Walker (1912–1993)
Education:	Bachelor's degree from Sarah Lawrence College
Spouse:	Mel Leventhal (1943–)
Date of Marriage:	March 17, 1967 (divorced in 1976)
Children:	Rebecca (1969–)

Further Reading

Altman, Linda Jacobs. *The American Civil Rights Movement: The African-American Struggle for Equality.* Springfield, N.J.: Enslow Publishers, 2004.

Kallen, Stuart A. *Women of the Civil Rights Movement.* Detroit: Lucent Books, 2005.

Lazo, Caroline. *Alice Walker: Freedom Writer.* Minneapolis: Lerner Publications, 2000.

McWhorter, Diane. *A Dream of Freedom: The Civil Rights Movement from 1954 to 1968.* New York: Scholastic Nonfiction, 2004.

Raatma, Lucia. *Alice Walker: African-American Author and Activist.* Chanhassen, Minn.: Child's World, 2004.

Look for more Signature Lives books about this era:

George Washington Carver: *Scientist, Inventor, and Teacher*

Hillary Rodham Clinton: *First Lady and Senator*

Amelia Earhart: *Legendary Aviator*

Dolores Huerta: *Labor Leader and Civil Rights Activist*

Langston Hughes: *The Voice of Harlem*

Wilma Mankiller: *Chief of the Cherokee Nation*

Thurgood Marshall: *Civil Rights Lawyer and Supreme Court Justice*

Elizabeth Cady Stanton: *Social Reformer*

Gloria Steinem: *Champion of Women's Rights*

Amy Tan: *Author and Storyteller*

Madam C.J. Walker: *Entrepreneur and Millionaire*

Booker T. Washington: *Innovative Educator*

On the Web

For more information on this topic, use FactHound.

1. Go to *www.facthound.com*
2. Type in this book ID: 0756534747
3. Click on the *Fetch It* button.

FactHound will find the best Web sites for you.

Historic Sites

California Hall of Fame
The California Museum for History, Women and the Arts
1020 O St.
Sacramento, CA 95814
916/653-7524
Exhibit showcases the contributions of Alice Walker and other Californians and offers biographical information, photographs, artifacts, and memorabilia

National Civil Rights Museum
450 Mulberry St.
Memphis, TN 38103
901/521-9699
Museum, converted from the motel where Martin Luther King Jr. was killed, contains exhibits on the key people and events of the civil rights movement

activism
action that is intended to bring about social or political change

advocate
someone who supports a person or ideal

anthropologist
person who studies human beings, including their physical characteristics and relationships with their environment and one another

deposition
legal reporting of someone's experience

dialect
variation in a language

feminist
someone who believes in the equality of women and men

folklorist
person who studies the customs, stories, sayings, dances, or art forms preseved among a people

mentor
adviser or teacher

segregated
when people of different races are kept separate from each other

sharecroppers
people who farmed land owned by others in exchange for housing and part of the profits

supremacists
people who believe one race is superior to another

Source Notes

Chapter 1

Page 10, line 20: *A Collaboration of Spirits: Casting and Acting "The Color Purple."* Warner Bros., 1985.

Page 11, line 3: Barbara Kramer. *Alice Walker: Author of The Color Purple.* Springfield, N.J.: Enslow Publishers, Inc., 1995, p. 6.

Chapter 2

Page 19, line 1: Alice Walker. "Beauty: When the Other Dancer is the Self." *In Search of Our Mothers' Gardens: Womanist Prose.* New York: Harcourt, Inc., 1983, p. 362.

Page 20, line 9: Ibid., p. 364.

Page 22, line 4: Alice Walker. Telephone interview. 6 Feb. 2007.

Page 23, line 1: Ibid.

Page 24, sidebar: Alice Walker. "The Black Writer and the Southern Experience." *In Search of Our Mothers' Gardens: Womanist Prose*, p. 27.

Page 24, line 6: *A Moment in Time: Conversations with Legendary Women—African American Women of Achievement.* Starlight Video, 2006.

Page 24, line 27: Alvin P. Sanoff. "The Craft of Survival." *U.S. News & World Report.* 3 June 1991, p. 51.

Page 25, line 10: Alice Walker. "Choosing to Stay at Home." *In Search of Our Mothers' Gardens: Womanist Prose*, p. 162.

Chapter 3

Page 28, sidebar: Alice Walker. Telephone interview. 6 Feb. 2007.

Page 28, line 27: Evelyn C. White. *Alice Walker: A Life.* New York: W.W. Norton & Company, 2004, p. 53.

Page 30, line 23: Ibid., p. 60.

Page 33, line 3: Ibid., p. 65.

Chapter 4

Page 36, line 26: Martin Luther King Jr. "I Have a Dream." American Rhetoric. 10 July 2007. www.americanrhetoric.com/speeches/mlkihaveadream.htm

Page 37, line 13: "Choosing to Stay at Home." *In Search of Our Mothers' Gardens: Womanist Prose*, p. 161.

Page 38, line 7: Alice Walker. "The Unglamorous but Worthwhile Duties of the Black Revolutionary Artist, or of the Black Writer Who Simply Works and Writes." *In Search of Our Mothers' Gardens: Womanist Prose*, p. 130.

Page 39, line 1: *Alice Walker: A Life*, p. 88.

Page 39, line 16: Ibid., p. 101.

Page 40, line 26: Alice Walker. Telephone interview. 6 Feb. 2007.

Chapter 5

Page 47, line 2: *Alice Walker: A Life*, p. 134.

Page 47, line 22: Ibid., p. 136.

Page 51, line 8: Alice Walker. Telephone interview. 6 Feb. 2007.

Page 51, line 26: Ibid.

Page 52, lines 17 and 21: Alice Walker. "The Civil Rights Movement: What Good Was It?" *In Search of Our Mothers' Gardens: Womanist Prose*, p. 151.

Page 53, line 1: *Alice Walker: A Life*, p. 152.

Page 53, line 9: Alice Walker. Telephone interview. 6 Feb. 2007.

Page 54, line 28: *Alice Walker: A Life*, p. 157.

Page 57, line 1: Alice Walker. "But Yet and Still the Cotton Gin Kept on Working." *In Search of Our Mothers' Gardens: Womanist Prose*, pp. 27, 28.

Chapter 6

Page 60, sidebar: Martin Luther King Jr. "I've Been to the Mountaintop." American Rhetoric. 10 July 2007. www.americanrhetoric.com/speeches/mlkivebeentothemountaintop.htm

Page 60, line 5: Alice Walker. "Coretta King: Revisited." *In Search of Our Mothers' Gardens: Womanist Prose*, p. 147.

Page 66, line 4: *Alice Walker: Author of The Color Purple*, p. 64.

Page 67, line 26: Alice Walker. *Good Night, Willie Lee, I'll See You in the Morning.* New York: Dial Press, 1979, p. 23.

Chapter 7

Page 71, line 10: Gregory Jaynes. "Living by the Word." *Life.* May 1989, p. 64.

Page 78, line 19: Evelyn C. White. "Alice's Wonderland." *Essence.* February 1996, p. 86.

Page 80, sidebar: *Alice Walker: A Life*, p. 377.

Chapter 8:

Page 84, line 21: *Alice Walker: A Life*, p. 406.

Page 85, line 7: Ibid.

Page 86, line 5: Charles Whitaker. "Alice Walker: Color Purple Author Confronts Her Critics and Talks About Her Provocative New Book." *Ebony.* May 1992, p. 86.

Page 87, line 1: "Alice's Wonderland," p. 84.

Page 87, line 9: Alice Walker. Telephone interview. 6 Feb. 2007.

Chapter 9

Page 92, line 1: Paula Giddings. "Alice Walker's Appeal." *Essence.* July 1992, p. 58.

Page 95, line 3: Alice Walker. Telephone interview. 6 Feb. 2007.

Select Bibliography

A Collaboration of Spirits: Casting and Acting "The Color Purple." Warner Bros., 2003.

Giddings, Paula. "Alice Walker's Appeal." *Essence.* July 1992.

Jaynes, Gregory. "Living by the Word." *Life.* May 1989.

Kramer, Barbara. *Alice Walker: Author of The Color Purple.* Springfield, N.J.: Enslow Publishers, Inc., 1995.

A Moment in Time: Conversations with Legendary Women—African American Women of Achievement. Starlight Video, 2006.

Sanoff, Alvin P. "The Craft of Survival." *U.S. News & World Report.* 3 June 1991.

Walker, Alice. *The Color Purple.* New York: Harcourt Brace Jovanovich, 1982.

Alice Walker. *Good Night, Willie Lee, I'll See You in the Morning.* New York: Dial Press, 1979.

Walker, Alice. *Horses Make a Landscape Look More Beautiful.* San Diego: Harcourt Brace Jovanovich, 1984.

Walker, Alice. *In Love and Trouble.* New York: Harcourt Brace Jovanovich, 1973.

Walker, Alice. *In Search of Our Mothers' Gardens: Womanist Prose.* New York: Harcourt, Inc., 1983.

Walker, Alice. *Living by the Word.* New York: Harcourt Brace Jovanovich, 1988.

Walker, Alice. *The Same River Twice: Honoring the Difficult.* New York: Scribner, 1996.

Walker, Alice. *We Are the Ones We Have Been Waiting For: Inner Light in a Time of Darkness.* New York: New Press, 2006.

Walker, Alice, and Pratibha Parmar. *Warrior Marks.* New York: Harcourt Brace, 1993.

Whitaker, Charles. "Alice Walker: Color Purple Author Confronts Her Critics and Talks About Her Provocative New Book." *Ebony.* May 1992.

White, Evelyn C. "Alice's Wonderland." *Essence.* February 1996.

White, Evelyn C. *Alice Walker: A Life.* New York: W.W. Norton & Company, 2004.

About the Author

Stephanie Fitzgerald has been writing nonfiction for children for more than 10 years. Her specialties include history, wildlife, and popular culture. Stephanie lives in Stamford, Connecticut, with her husband, Brian, and daughter, Molly.

Image Credits

Peter Kramer/Getty Images, cover (top), 4–5, 94; AP Photo/Noah Berger, cover (bottom), 2, 88, 101 (top); Courtesy of Alice Walker, photo by Robert Allen, 8, 74, 79; Photos 12/Alamy, 11, 87, 100 (top right); Marion Post Wolcott/Library of Congress/Getty Images, 13; Content Mine International/Alamy, 15; Courtesy of Alice Walker, 16, 64, 68, 81, 96 (top left), 98 (top left); Library of Congress, 18, 97 (bottom), 98 (bottom right), 101 (bottom left); Courtesy of Alice Walker, photo by John Peck, 21, 77, 100 (top left); AP Photo, 23, 31, 34, 48, 61; Robert W. Kelley/Time Life Pictures/Getty Images, 26; John Loengard/Time Life Pictures/Getty Images, 29; Bettmann/Corbis, 33, 46, 58; Hulton Archive/Getty Images, 37; Courtesy of Alice Walker, photo by Staughton Lynd, 38, 96 (top right); Courtesy of Alice Walker, photo by Dana Durst, 41; Oscar White/Corbis, 42; Flip Schulke/Corbis, 44, 53; Ambient Images/Alamy, 50; Courtesy of Alice Walker, photo by Renee, 56, 97 (top); Wikipedia, public-domain image, 63; Norma G. Chambers/Shutterstock, 66; Cover of "The Color Purple" by Alice Walker, published by Harcourt Brace Jovanovich, 70, 99 (top); Courtesy of Alice Walker, photo by Joanna Maccario, 73, 98 (top); AP Photo/Gordon Parks, 82; Everett Collection/Rex USA, 85; Courtesy of Alice Walker, photo by Susan Kirschner, 90; Franklin D. Roosevelt Presidential Library & Museum, 96 (bottom left); Corel, 96 (bottom middle); NASA, 96 (bottom right), 98 (bottom left), 100 (bottom); Courtesy Intel Museum Archives and Collections, 98 (bottom middle); Keystone/Getty Images, 99 (bottom left); Svetlana Zhurkin, 99 (bottom right); DigitalVision, 101 (bottom right).